THE TETHERED MAN

The Tethered Man

Poems
by

LAZAR SARNA

Adelaide Books
New York / Lisbon
2019

THE TETHERED MAN
Poems
By Lazar Sarna

Published by Adelaide Books, New York / Lisbon
adelaidebooks.org
Editor-in-Chief
Stevan V. Nikolic

For any information, please address Adelaide Books
at info@adelaidebooks.org
or write to:
Adelaide Books
244 Fifth Ave. Suite D27
New York, NY, 10001

ISBN-10: 1-951214-50-1
ISBN-13: 978-1-951214-50-0

Printed in the United States of America

To my Jewel, whose perception of life matches mine.

Contents

Introduction to
The Tethered Man

The tethered man (*adnei ha-sadeh*) is described as a human-like creature connected to the earth by an umbilical cord. It dies if the cord were cut, since that is its essential channel for food. *Adnei ha-sadeh* literally means master of the field.

In ancient and medieval legends, the *adnei ha-sadeh* is humanoid, or an ape, or a plant-man. The creature is also known as the *yadua*, a wild tethered man capable of speaking but in unintelligible sounds (see chapter 8:5 of *Tractate Kilayim*)

It is hunted by shooting arrows or spears at its cord, or taunting it to dart away from its point of connection until it yanks and snaps the cord.

The creature's bones are said to be an aid to fortune-telling and communication with the dead, by placing them in the arm-pit of the seer or mouth of a corpse.

The *adnei ha-sadeh* is either extinct or lives in the wild regions of the earth, or never existed at all.

THE TETHERED MAN

Like A Beak

Like a beak out of a bird's face
out of his belly shoots a cord
thick as a banana tree's waist
meshed in the soil
defiantly anchored as a boulder's mind;
he knows the circumference
his tether has imposed.

Yet this is normal for a man-plant
because only the rootless can walk away
into a world far more hostile
than the familiar
where they think
no one wants to eat them
or at least torture them for their oddity.

Had he been born an eagle-plant
His reputation as a predator
Would have brought him invitations
To meals of some one else's carrion
Instead of hourly tests of his bland resistence.

Breakfast Is The Best Meal

Breakfast is the best meal

By regurgitating dew dripping from his forehead
he can manufacture a very mild wine
which goes well with whatever his cord brings him

When a fog squatted one day,
he swallowed it whole
like a snake's snack

But there was nothing in his rasping stomach
except a wondrous thought
that life brings satiety if least expected

His body, so connected to the ground
was the philosopher, not his ripening brain
That is why he stifled the big queries and their answers.
Neither were digestible
and rotted away in the earth if stored.

One Arrogant Wednesday

One arrogant Wednesday
he gave himself names with hard human consonants
titles excelling as prefixes
numbers as suffixes

With no-one to call him or mispronounce
if they did;
why would it matter what sound
he answered to
unless it was a twig crashing in the darkened bush
or the hum of a meeting of carnivores deciding their meal.

Thursday came,
a theoretical day
when everything and everyone could be important
so his fears and face were named;
his lack of clothing, his grunting and hopping
most things about him
came to be known by what they were.

Looking Closely

Looking closely at his tether
causes blindness of the retina:
whatever is left of the eye
can still see and even hear.

Something
causes a malfunction of light
because of the man's nakedness.
His cord is so embarrassing
it becomes his private part
available for idle glancing, as if it were in solar eclipse.

A sign should be posted
special glasses should be worn
fines should be levied
a science of judges should be convened
if anyone dares to stare
and worse still,
point.

A tether is anything that grabs the optic nerves
like the seat in an out-of-control car, or
a noose that hangs the innocent and guilty
from the inside of their breathing
like a flight down the elevator shaft.

It is there when you feel it,
even there when insensible.

More than a patch that merely covers
More than a dream that merely disguises.
More like a phantom limb.
More like the leash of a dog with a cellphone in its mouth,
both running away from a cruel and ever-babbling master.

The Only Way

The best way to know
If it is a plant or person is to transplant
Like we did to the vegetable sheep.

We would have to dig up
A generous plate of ground
To get at the base of the stalk
And see if it takes root in another garden.

If it does not respond to sweet water and fat soil
Within a few days
Or if it wilts in transit out of
Fear or homesickness
We can draw our differing conclusions.

The only other way (not recommended)
Is to suck its sap
The same way it pulls water from below its feet.
If its juice is heavy and sweet
You greatly mistook the fruit for the plant.

He Thought

He thought he owned the earth
that it was another one of his heads.

It had no nervous system
he could interpret
so he thought it did not need one.

A gravity-sucking mass
his dumb other self.
This globe he pulled was
a prisoner's iron ball
except that he was commanding
what it should weigh.

The minerials, liquids and turds
stuck on
were conversation pieces for his own complaining,
not for others
who could not care less
if an intimate part of him
exposed
looked like a pathologist's interesting nightmare.

After Absorbing

After absorbing a stale stalk of celery
he was exposed to the rock-and-roll
of its juices:
ulcerating tunes in his stomach
transformed him into
teenaged lips
looking for a first love.

He could understand a tune
distinct from the food it came in;
and so he could only hum and grunt
with his mouth full.

If he had understood rhythm,
he could have been able to count
and then recognize he was subject to time
like the daily willing greens around him.

Someone Made Him Think War

Someone made him think war
was another word for square dancing
When everyone lines up in a pattern
And follows the rasping calls of the leader
in sync with thumping musics.

It was a hoax by weasels and crows
Knowing that he could neither dance
nor fathom what it was like
To prance free of a tether
remaining restricted to the square.
They would whisper through their fur
or clap their black feathers all night
To create the image of a rumour he could swallow.

Not that he could know what an argument
through artillery was,
Nor if death was possible by means
other than shriveling for want of water.
He seemed to understand the march of skeletons wearing helmets,
Although he had no bones to see or feel.

War had its limitations,
That's all he could understand.

In His Mind

In his mind, although invited to play in a string quartet,
he refuses because he cannot find his cello.
It makes him nervous to think it was stolen,
and with it, his passion for being elsewhere.

He has said no before,
saying invitations were half-hearted,
or that he would never get to rehearsals on time,
let alone opening night.

Anyway, he does not think much of fellow musicians,
petty, acerbic.
He would have to stand awkwardly
to play a cello with a protuberance
from his belly.

Why don't you try the oboe,
they would smirk helpfully.

He explained to the caucus of grass
Growing around him
He could never be the leader
Because he could not read nor hear.
He thought his eyes had to be the shape of an 'E'
In order to read 'E'.
He thought his ear had to look like chord to hear it.

A leader had to break though silence
To make a written speech
To lead a symphonic theme
So that everyone would follow.
His only communicable talent was waiting.

Anyway, he had nowhere to lead them except to his spot.
That was already taken.

A Beetle

A beetle with multiple mandibles
And audible blood hot for attack
is not a reason to call 911,
Even if the insect will tear at his heart
and leave him destroyed.

A downpour of crashed clouds
Targeting only his existence
will not bring out first responders.

Even a cataclysmic escape of bestiaries
from a lax zoo heading his way
Is not as urgent as a heart attack on Fifth Avenue
Or scattered bones and blood on a highway overpass
Where crowds have gathered
or traffic has congealed
like a gelatin dessert.

The worth of a being is measured by their urgencies
He found out when his panic
Of eventually dying
Overtook his eyes, blocked his face
And caused him to cry
For what others mistook as help.

He Would Not Fare Well

He would not fare well
At a job interview.
No prior experience in sales or administration.
No community work or letter of recommendation.
He would not sit still
Or stand erect when answering questions.
He could not chair a meeting
Using his gurgling voice as authoritative.
Asked about his favourite animal,
He would say he was afraid of them all.
As to colour, he would favour
The green tint of his fingers.

He would be late
Or never show up at all.
Whether he showed or not,
In the end,
The job would already have been filled
By someone even less qualified.

He Has A Vow

He has a vow from trees
That they will not manufacture fruit
Nor window-dress their leaves
While he is absent for any reason.

Once he returns,
They may circulate their syrups
and arrange their foliage and buds
like vendors at their market kiosques.

He, though, is not going anywhere
Except for moments of distraction.
His day dream is the same
As a vacation.
During that time away,
he fears he will miss
what everyone else experiences,
those unimportant moments
when great sales take place
and earthquakes prepare
to redecorate the earth.

The Tethered Man Gives No Commitments

The tethered man gives no commitments.
He is not a sycamore
Although so many want to feel his bark out of curiosity.

Anyway, he knows where to hide if he were in default.
Hiding means jumping all over the place
Like an unsettled stomach.

He gives no promises, no forwarding address,
Nothing that would tie him tomorrow
Not even the footprint he left behind today.
Any word he might have given a minute ago
Has already turned to spittle.
Any affidavit he solemnly swore
Has creased like the skin of his cheeks.

That dry spot
Where a tiger squatted
Was where a tethered woman stalk
Was growing one foot, two feet
Until its leaf shaped like an oversized hip
Folded into itself
Along its alimentary vein.

He could see what was happening.
Non-committal, not willing to display a yearning
The tethered man did what all nurses do
For the chronically ill:

Record their deterioration,
Whisper a word of hope,
Make sure, according to a chart,
They are all comfortable to the end.

A Toy Must Have Fallen

A toy must have fallen from the sky
not far from his larger toe.

Since then he thinks
everyone has a painted-on face
and badly fitting joints that disconnect,
or a lost wind-up key
and dead batteries as a spine.

How marvelous, he dreams,
to give life to a thing
born to play
only if a spirit comes.

Among His Chores

Among his chores, conversation,
beginning abruptly and so ending
since words hurt him.
They made him fidget.

He would believe a falcon
about the end of days
because of its overview and clean feathers

He could not believe a salmon
even about the mundane
because he did not know fish.

The improbability of
so much water in a sea
and its creatures
without use for land
was one of the few things that made him guffaw,
and bring it into his speech.

And once in a sarcastic mood,
the helpless yawn of a tree
after the crack of a branch breaking
became his laughter.

His Circle

His circle so rank with gibberish and sweat.

No one goes near
except to kill or taunt
Friendship is not on the menu
as is the sludge
rolling through his tether.

Nothing to share, appease, console or enlighten
the give-and-take of comrades
is something you and he excrete or ache.

Around Him

Around him, vegetation withered
like bad questions,
insects fell dead from the sky;
yet grandchildren of orchids
and wasps grew in their place
without his ever asking
if he would live forever.

Once a lifeless chick hit him in one eye.
The other eye, usually bulbous
squinted in fear of going blind too
That fear sent him running crazily in one direction
to tear his cord
and learn what would be
if he were no more.

His Complexion

his complexion has the sheen of a used punching bag

does he rub his face against peaches
so that their fuzz can matte against his

his complexion has the low lustre of a sardine can

do his fishermen never jettison drag lines
so that their catch of his lips is massive

or if the violence of the times is personal to him
does he cry when the net scoops up the whole sea

his complexion has the down of a dog's tennis ball

does he have a tail that conducts like a baton
so that any orchestra would be dizzy

my complexion has the light of a bent moon
an easy match for the masks of his

my complexion is actually made of skin,
feels like it, ages like it,
the type that planets use for nightly shows

We Say, Go To Sleep

We say, go to sleep
But we do not mean it is a place to go to.

You do not sleep because you do not travel
Or are just afraid of being eaten
Or expanded upon by dreams.

Even if sleep were a direction rather than a place
All your compasses end in borders
Like an old green radar screen
Where you are a bug-sized blip

If you could fly instead of just lunging upward
Your tether would haul you
Like a predator starting on you for breakfast

Sleep is a place to point to
Like a community where no-one worries
his ground will turn to mud
And the roots of his feet up-end and dry.
You are not neighbourly.

He Has No House

He has no house,
yet he detects something more than his breath
or the plumbing's parts
moving within it.

He wishes he were secure under the blankets
which do not exist.
Now he is exposed
to the movement of the world's fears.

Without a house, how did the ancients
in their windowless visions
deal with the volcano's rumble
or an enemy's war chant:
maybe by sleeping too deeply
or by the substitution of prophecies
for what was to become
the destruction of their civilization.

Without a house, he is the address:
that much he established after fighting with the postman.
He is not really a resident,
more like a vicinity person,
just there, not reachable
like a flailing flag on a rusting pole
or a constant tire screech
due to poor urban planning.

He Discovered

He discovered he had xylem bones,
proof that he was not a vegetable.

He also discovered they were magic
if placed in the right hands.

As to who put them inside his chest and arms
and how he could take them out
and what sorcery would arise,
he could not tell by feeling his body.

The marvelling he endured was enough to force a dream
of vortexes and constellations
he thought of one day visiting.

As A Pet

The project of turning him into a pet
requires his stalk to be cut,
and his throat to accomodate a dog's howl.

Even if possible,
we would have to tie him to the cement
bench outside the supermarket
while we shop,
convince the other condo owners
he will not tear up the lobby couch.

When we go to work and leave him alone
in the den, he will remember being alone,
except this time: we have programmed the
screen to teach him many musics.

He must refuse to poke through trash
on early morning walks,
and not fear the territorial pee of what
he might think are wolves.
Eventually, he will adopt a gratitude face
To mask his wilderness.

It is a dream to think he would accept another home,
even if it has central air
and is listed among the 10% most desirable mansions
in the country,
where butlers keep knives in their uniforms for protection.

Search And Recovery

Search and recovery means looking below
the ice on the lake in the dark undercurrent
with its swift music
for someone whose hair is standing dead up
maybe eyes awake in frost,
and reaching until touching
then pulling up a very callous weight
to the opening in the surface.

How can you search in ice,
man on a stalk?
How can you even hope to come running
When someone calls in fright
And slips into a cold paradise?

When The Time Comes

When the times comes for his demise,
whether by withering with the new season
or crisping and flaking like a veteran piece of bark,
he will have the same blank stare
you see on a frog being swallowed whole by a viper
or a lottery winner just announced.

That stare means flight of the mind upward
to nowhere special
no gravity, no seatbelts
nothing anticipated, nothing lost,
the same complete serenity of a tree
seconds before you hear someone shouting,
Timber.

Remember The Face

Remember the face of the pilot
Who unintentionally dropped a nuclear bomb over Montana
During a training mission.
His first eyes asked, Who me? Did it explode?

Like the tethered man's face
Dazed by the unintentionality of the
damage others think he causes
By the zinging of his elastic leaps
He is reminiscent of a major bomb falling without target
On bystanders enjoying fried ice cream.

His only mission is himself, he implies by his strangeness.
He is training to live a longer life, but
What wouldn't a four-star chef give to gather
him after he splats on the ground
Or a vegetable cart pusher forfeit to catch him mid-air.

Some Speculate

Some speculate that in hyper-frigid air
He could crystallize and shatter into pre-cut diamonds.
It would prove his essence was high-society,
bound for necklaces and weddings rings.

But then it would take his absolute demise to prove a point.
A better way would be to concentrate on
the mini-silky protruberances
Covering his skin
Creating a shimmer changing with each angle.
That would prove he is not averse to
current colour and fashion,
and the search for self-expansion.

If only the rope would leave him alone.

If He Were A Tailor

If he were a tailor,
Every made-to-measure suit
Would have a gaping aperture
In the centre of the jacket and trouser waist
To accommodate the tether:
That is not what the customer wants or needs.

If he were an Olympic athletic trainer
He would have shot-putters and
Synchronized swimmers
Leaping, twirling, screeching
Running in circles:
Not what they need to qualify, let alone win.

If he opened franchised restaurants
Catering to other *adnei ha-sadeh,*
How could they possibly come to any of his locations
Unless he delivered to their locations,
If he could find any of them.

If he were reduced to unemployment,
After serious attempts at a business jackpot,
At least he could claim he was an entrepreneur who lies
in wait for the next boom and the next investor
With great dreams and gobs of other people's money.

Someone Once Heard

Someone once heard him say:
A language is not foreign if you speak it.

Another heard him say otherwise:
Where there is food, there is no need for justice.

Yet another claimed he heard:
Solitude needs no justification.

One more reported his saying:
The end of any conflict is sad.

Why would he bother with aphorisms
when he never encountered
the concept of truth
or the satisfaction it brings to those
who have nothing else to be proud of.

His Idea Of Dancing

His idea of dancing is shoving.

Music only inspires him
to see the earth beneath as his partner
who does not syncopate easily
with another's beat.

How he would like to find the waist of the globe
to hold it in rhythm
in a ballroom swirl,
to be known as suave
rather than for his two left feet.

He Will Never Feel

He will never feel the joy of
catching the last bus to far away
not paying attention in class
or winning at Scrabble with the word zee.

He is more likely to find sorrow in
attracting a screech of crazed hyenas
having no sense of gourmet dining
showing little for his life but sweat

What more can be expected from a tied-down cursed;
how more sweet can you make a eulogy.

His mutilated body
would be cole slaw;
his legacy to expectant heirs would
have to be himself as food.
As an inter-generational transition
no-one would scowl once lunch was served.

A Jail

A jail has an inside and an outside.
His jail has a radius he likes to call
His warden.

As for escaping
Most prisoners end up in a swamp
Chased by blood-hounds.
Covered in leaves and leeches,
They fill their eyes with mosquitoes and
Lose their shoes in quicksand.
Then someone makes a movie
Out of the caper.

They have a reason to
Scrape their way of out their cement cells.
He has no reason,
And anyway, no helping accomplices
Who owe him so much abiding love
They would gladly muddy their brand new jeans.

Unfair

Unfair to ask him
if he can love two at once
with the same intensity
when he is ineluctably committed to his cord
for food and identity.

Call it an obsession if not love.

Would he leave it for another
if he had the choice.
Would he plant someone else
in his belly and assume
his sustenance would flow by reflex.

That person would have to be
worse than a slave,
worse than a hose full of slushy nutrients.

That someone would have to be better
than what he has
maybe by the touch
or by words he never heard pronounced before.

The Messenger

If no one is home,
the messenger of death
seeps in through the keyhole and
foundation cracks.

It leaves Post-Its
near the toaster, bathroom sink
and sock drawer
with no return address.

If the victim does answer the door,
he thinks no one rang the bell.
Pranked, he simmers until he takes a bath
to relax.
He does not rise up again.

The tethered man has no doorbell
nor place to host a single Post-It.
Maybe that explains it:
when the time and messenger come
those close by hear background drums
like death rattles
or crinkling noises.

The process
of shriveling into a desiccated stalk begins,

which some would call
the blooming of a dried clutch of chrysanthemum.

The wind then blows to extinguish any live ember,
cooling this stand of straw.

Ask if this is now indistinguishable from
a faded remnant of a far gone season.

A Tree Is Snoring

A tree is snoring
from the armpit of its branches
in the grove on his perimeter.

What can he do to stop it,
assuming he could find
where that vicious hand-saw
of a noise is coming from.

Night after night
the monkeys, sloths, toucans
complain they are sleep-deprived.
You can tell from their bleary eyes
and watery casts they leave behind
in a drip down the bark.

This becomes the impetus for their prayer,
that lightning should strike
in such a surgical way
as to shut up the tree's throat.

Let it be accountable for its failure
to spread its twigs like lace
in an etiquette fit for
one of the tallest beings
in the world.

He Fell In Love

He fell in love with a stalk of jungle corn
That sprouted one night without warning
Within arms' reach.

The tassels were reminiscent of a woman's yoo-hoo.
It waved its hand-sized leaves at him non-stop
Like an air-raid warning flag.

He could not eat.
His teeth had interspersed splinters of joy
He yearned to brag;
He was loved in return.

Within a week
Two baby sprouts shot up
Like a stand-still family.
He handed out grass blades like cigars.
If only he could think of fitting names
That would last the season

Too soon, they all wilted while he did not.
He could not prevent the onset of rust.
Whatever tears he fashioned
Were not the medicine they needed.
They needed him not to mourn
Not even to notice they had come.

He Heard

He heard waves have arthritis:
They crash their bloated joints against rocks to ease the pain.
Of course, these days you can't trust
Anything people say because they say
Anything to gain your trust by commiserating.

Plants have no pain, he heard,
Which is why he thinks he is a person.
What he feels must be pain
Although he has nothing to compare it to.

He would ask a wave if he saw one,
Why do you smash, why do you roll.
Maybe it is the lunar pull,
Not the ache of being alive.

He has seen wavelets in a puddle before his stalk,
agitated by the wind
like sardines scattering before a shark.

Maybe a puddle is the sea
Exaggerated by all the liars around him.
Maybe it does have pain
So slight it is not worth noticing.

His Ten By Ten Corral

His ten by ten corral might seem
A dust and leaf-bit box.

If we can trust it,
The eye of a crow sees his microscopic grid lines
Of safe and unsafe streets,
One hundred and two strip malls,
Scores of light industrial zones and bowling alleys,
Thirty cultural and gathering places
Restaurants and dancing strips with plenty of parking,
One court house and two jails
Bath houses, a soccer stadium
And one hilltop for broadcasting antennae.

Every mind is a city.
Not everyone is a crow.

Although There Is Not Enough Space

Although there is not enough space to be reckless
That does not mean
He could not have an outrageous meal
Of stray dogs.

Reckless means driving a truck
In the wrong lane with the doors open,
Running through a glass pane
Just to hear the crack
Which for him is not possible.

He has the virtues of a model citizen,
Does not litter
Pays no taxes if not due
Does not disturb the sleep of the vicinity
Or the moon.

Yes, he does exercise his right to vote
By thinking good thoughts.
Some even want him to run for public office
Many, many years from now.

A Confusion

A confusion of wild turkeys
Some with small heads but bigger brains
Descended near his stalk
To discuss leadership matters before invading the brush.

He let them stay by freezing his motion,
by making as if he were a hardened shoot.
Several of them with larger heads
Pecked at his tether out of curiosity
To gage its rubberiness.

Unwilling to be wounded for nothing in return
He unfroze and expanded into the image
Of a vulturous savage with full sound effects.
They scattered, leaving around his stalk
The dense untidy manure they had been holding in.

With no-one for days to clean it up,
His stalk was fertilized and his mind took on new energy.
His vision sharpened.
He became oblivious to being sedentary.
He wanted to melt the bushes as if he were lava.
He recognized new muscles, grew heavy bowels.
There was gravel in his voice.

Just as he was about to state his identity
After a week of surge,
The rain and wind washed the ground clean.
He could sense his drains evacuating what he thought
Would never go away nor come again.

Along His Funeral Path

Along his funeral path
Will sit the mud mouse
spontaneously generated from wet dirt
the week before.

The vegetable lamb,
Growing on a stalk
in a small patch just beyond his vision,
Will take its place amid tall grasses.

The tree geese developing from branches
still blanketed by their leaf skins and freshly fallen
will squat behind them in a nervous circle.

Whether an animal-turned-plant
Or vice versa
These are his generation fortunate enough to have an essence of life
That will stretch longer than his.
They now practice odes
While he will have turned into particles of a twig.

I WON'T BE GOING TO MARS

I Won't Be Going To Mars

I won't be going to Mars this week-end.
The little life there may be does not know how to play bridge.

Now that the riff-raff have discovered it,
I don't want to share a planet
with street vendors and middle-managers.

I prefer my time on the balcony,
above the tops of heads, and bad cooking smells.

If I happen to sing about being so high up
without melody or beat or words,
my only possible audience is a deaf horizon.

Walls Don't Wait

Walls don't wait with you in a room.
They have their own reason to be patient.

If you were waiting in a capsule zooming to Mars
The walls would be with you
Until they peeled off
Leaving you thinking that
Waiting with tension
Is not the same as hanging around
Hoping to be called next by the nurse.

Tension has no other purpose
Than to bully your sweat glands.
If the red planet were to appear in the window,
Even though the mission would look almost complete
You would not be waiting to land.
You would be in panic that you left your passport
In the drawer of your bad bow ties.

Either Planets

Either planets are so huge
they fill up a room
and cut off the possibility of conversation;

Or they are so small
they fall off the table
to get sucked up with crumbs
by the vacuum cleaner.

The mid-sized ones
are uncomfortable
in a salon setting.
They prefer to stay outside
where the stars keep shooting
until breakfast arrives.

A good host will proclaim:
there is room for everyone.

For those who dispute this cordial fact
let them try to resist
buttered toast
and hot chocolate
served on the eve of a lunar eclipse.

King Of Mars

The first astronaut to land went rogue
declaring himself King of Mars.
Mission control could not reach him for days
while he wandered far away
to name plains, cliffs, boulders and valleys
after himself.

When Earth finally contacted him
he held it in contempt with banishment
for doubting the prerogative
that Royalty can do no wrong.

With no-one to question his divine origin
he assembled the creatures of vast emptiness
to confirm that
were the King to die, they should shout to the galaxy,
Long live the King.

Days were busy erecting obelisks
sculpting giant pyramidal heads of himself
inventing a novel hieroglyphic language he spoke to his court
inducting the sun and the earth into his pantheon of assistants.

All the beneficent decrees he issued
all the goodwill he spread during his short reign
he knew he would have to leave
to the landing crew in the succeeding dynasty
with a taste of futility
once his earthly and very common food and water
would abruptly leak and quickly expire.

My Mandatory Team

My mandatory team
Was to be
A fig-drier
Who insisted
his fruit was better than the carob

And
A water-skin carrier
Who had never tasted what he bore,
had no interest until it was empty

And
A hyssop trimmer
Who knew his leaves had more magic than
A solar system.

I was the parochial captain,
My mind so fixed on not getting there
And not returning the same way.

Yes

Yes,
About that added strength
My fingers have achieved
As I hang on to the left wing
Of the airplane,

Or
About my broadening chest
As I try to avoid the crush
Of two Arabian stallions
Sleeping in my shipping container.

I will answer all questions
About my travel habits
Once I let go of the spider silk
Stuck to the mid-section
Of the George Washington Bridge.

Must Be A Better Place

Must be a better place for a cigarette butt
Than in her thinly concocted lips
That will suck it in, send it to her stomach
Full of decayed inventory.

He thought, if she were a Martian
She would work in a spitoon factory
Making exports for the universe
Of bad digestion.

That's what her people do best, or worst,
manufacture shiney objects out of rare minerals
package them in anti-gravitational foil
to delight enormous stars
before they burst.

Then they lost curiosity in each other
because snooping on their intimate emails
was no longer interesting:
They were forwarding left-over flaming phrases
from old love letters to new suitors.

There was no option.
Having fatigued their own love
they thought
no-one would know any better on-line

Another way would have been
to invite all hackers
to use their sharpest algorythms
to create a billion hits,
leave the impression
that everyone in the world
for one nano-second
was willing to intervene.

Either Planets

Either planets are so huge
they fill up a room
and cut off the possibility of conversation;

Or they are so small
they fall off the table
to get sucked up with crumbs
by the vacuum cleaner.

The mid-sized ones
are uncomfortable
in a salon setting.
They prefer to stay outside
where the stars keep shooting
until breakfast arrives.

A good host will proclaim:
there is room for everyone.

For those who dispute this cordial fact
let them try to resist
buttered toast
and hot chocolate
served on the eve of a lunar eclipse.

From Behind

From behind,
The leader of this planet
Would look like a seven foot tall shrimp
With the shadow of muck waving
from translucent tentacles.

I would be afraid of staring
because he might have eyes in his elbows.
I would be more afraid that he would turn around,
demonstrate an indigestible ugliness.

No, he would rotate.
He would have a Cary Grant square-jawed face.
More off-setting would be his wrinkle-free
Grey suit
And Bristol accent
Not befitting someone
in charge of a vast cruel desert.

Distance, Like Old Thick Cheese

Distance, like old thick cheese,
has to be nibbled, not confronted
unless there is a way to completely ingest
miles on end
without a gulp.

I know someone
who would eat the shavings
off a round of gouda
yet talk to each one of them
before they touched his lips.

He was not in a hurry,
nor did he think he should offend
the cheese just to admit
to the upper classes
he was unable to deal with hunger.

Mars Police

Mars police would not give you
A ticket for a seat-belt infraction
Just to have you bribe them,
Although they have no law
that does not prevent them
from being honest.

Then how do they occupy themselves?

They spread good cheer
By telling visitors to come again,
And persuading those bent on
Gratuitous vandalism
To look to their inner selves
As the ultimate victims.

One day there will be no need for them.
They will have to retire
With a modest pension
And give up the very uniforms that brought
Joy to even the most hardened criminal.

In One Dimension

In one dimension
you were dancing on top of Table 6
at the wedding reception
oblivious to your knee problem,
other invitees' plates and gravity.

In my home dimension,
I contended with multiple calls from a problem relative,
barging door knockings by charity beggars,
and the honey bees in the fat faces of the hibiscus.

Where was I to dance
if I was forced to hide under the dining room table
until the band went away?

Until The Ambulance

Until the ambulance came
He saw what he thought was his last sunrise.
He had never had much of a relationship with sunrises,
And this may have been his first.

The chair he slouched in
Saved only for guests because of its soft suede,
Never allowed guests for fear of dusty pants.

The rouge of the sunrise softened the chair even more.
The sudden staccato red of the ambulance lights
Was sending a dusty code.

When he was lifted and carried out
The sun sought other places and lives.
The chair recovering from the slouch
Had open arms and no more restrictions.

THE FREEDOM

Love Poems

Love poems talk about people
who cannot sit still
long enough to love.

Compare a shopping list
composed by two
who want to eat together.

Asparagus is on the list
after an anguished debate
over freshness:
the same with ciabatta rolls.

These list makers realize
It is time to
stop moving around
long enough to decide
if they want to bond or leave,
serve a green salad or starve
chew alone or swallow in questionable company.

I Bought A Grocery

I bought a grocery of stale milks.
I needed to say I was in retail
To impress you with my inventory.

Then I bought a building of sticks.
I needed to say I was in real estate
To show you I had brittle insight.

Then I bought a bank of seasons.
I needed to say I was in time
To vaunt that I could regret the autumn.

And now at the turning point in my career
I will buy unused woods and plains that need paths
To show you overgrowth in my investments.

Nobody Likes To Fall

Nobody likes to fall
especially droplets of rain
when they ping against tin umbrellas.

Do they jump or are they pushed?

In torrents, they must jump because of the anger.
In scattered showers
minding their own business in a cloud,
they must be pushed under duress
by a madman fond of puddles.

Maybe it's all horseplay,
a stupid moment when falling from the sky
without a parachute
must mean they believe they will live again.

Beach Day

Beach day for a sun with nothing to do;
miles of cheap sand
delivered by a discount warehouse:
all you want to do is sleep
where there was never any shade.
At least chain yourself to driftwood
so that neither of you is stolen.

I bet everyone on shore
has lousy diatribes and bathing suits with holes.
I bet the waves are pasted to the water
like a used vaudeville backdrop.

Wake up when your dream is over.
Wake up when the tide comes calling for its welfare.

I Needed A Button

I needed a button the day after
the button store closed.
I never missed a button before.
My suit will be embarrassed.

I needed milk a week after
most cows went mad.
I thought I could do without milk.
Yet my coffee will have no texture.

I need so much
years after everyone else seems complacent.
I thought I could get along with nothing.
No-one can get along with nothing.

She Went Out With Someone Postal

She went out with someone postal
to please her mother.

They had coffee that did not lead anywhere.

He called after for a reprise.
She said no
although he seemed okay but not her type.

Years later watching TV
She saw him carted away after killing co-workers.
She phoned her mother to say he could
have been her son-in-law.

Her mother did not know
what she was talking about.

Very Bad And Guilty People

very bad and guilty people
are often tied to trees
on a precipice about to crumble
into an active volcano,
erupting every three hundred years
when indignation causes the earth
to wake from its happiness

very bad and guiltypeople
have dry-cleaned skin
because they have no water
to fill their pores;
no reminder to apologize
to their kidnappees

why do they bother being born:
the core of the earth will flame
without them,
the ice of the world will still harden with joy

My Rescue Team

My rescue team has saved
A sitter in a worn-out suit
From a worn-out couch

It has won praise for driving dogs
Away from prize flowers

Its greatest achievement to date
is refusing involvement in the anger
at supermarket line-ups
and the shame of missing bargains

Those who are facing avalanches
Those who cannot control the sea
Those who cannot find a reason for living another day
Should not rely too heavily on us

They are better off keeping a diary
While the light and their strength last

I Am Concerned About Large Animals

I am concerned about large animals
With small brains.

If a predator were to do them a favour
By not stalking one day,
The overwhelming question, Why,
Would flood their few brain cells
Leaving no space to calculate daily needs.

Why would be so momentous a problem
They could never solve,
They would slowly stop their simply routines
Fall on their ribs,
Lie as a welcoming prey for something
hidden, hungry and less merciful.

He Married The Daughter Of A Snake

He married the daughter of a snake.
She had one hundred siblings who did not survive their birth.
For forty years, he feared she might bite him.
At the end, she squeezed him in an amorous crush
terminating his concern.

She married the son of a camel.
He promised he could not spit more than a few inches
And that his hooves did not contain gelatin used in most soups.
For years she saw him progressively walk with a bent
Much resembling a hump
But not two.

It is not possible to marry out of the human race
Without feeling requirements are not being fulfilled.
To make an animal into a consort
Would make a mockery out of in-laws.

On the other hand, to husband a thought or a sound
Would make us search
a very long time
for an explanation.

One Hot Garden Day

One hot garden day
I painted the sunflowers black
so that the squirrels and raccoons
could not see them.
They over-painted them green
and ate them like apples.

The red cardinal switched colours
with the monarch butterfly
so he could turn into a leopard
which he did to stalk and impress his mate.
The butterfly, now thoroughly crimson,
held court for all the complainants
about the insolent gardener.

This Used To Be

This used to be a quiet neighbourhood.
Then someone stabbed a teenager on Knife Drive
Near Ocean Road where a great-grandfather
almost drowned in the bath.
The woman who won the lottery
used to live on Loser Lane
until her husband and brother
gambled away her money.

The streets are not safe anymore.

It is no better in the wealthy area of town
where Bank meets Gold Boulevard.

No better in the surrounding woods
where paths have no name or direction.

No better in the hollow of hills
where bears no longer snore their whereabouts.

No better on the lips of the sea
that used to tell which way is east,
which is west.

If I Could See

If I could see out of the corner of my eye,
My eye would not be round.

Limbs cannot be pointed,
except an argumentative finger.

In order for organs to fit,
They must be rounded and baggy
Like an over-soaked nut.

Everything of the body must make a good first impression.

We Went To The Wrong Funeral

We went to the wrong funeral
wrong little lady also called Mary.

But we stayed and learned from the emoting grandchild
that she had an even more interesting life
with different sorrows and energies
as if we now knew her, or could have easily known her
to the exclusion of the other Mary
who, for all we can gather, may still be alive.

On the way back,
The bus is empty
Through no fault of its own,
So is the bathtub
Same with the library shelf
And the Grand Canyon.

No-one's fault if it's preferable that way,
If that's what time and place want,
If that's what make emptiness
feel much better.

Help Wanted

He lost his job as a body guard
For a despicable ruler.
Overslept during the assassination.

And before that, as a wine taster
For a man on death row.
Wasn't thirsty when clemency was refused.

And before that, as an X-ray technician
For a boneless man.
Nothing to see when he complained.

And before that, as a trainer
For an aimless bird.
He never took flight when the flock called.

I Knew A Dog Like Her

I knew a dog like her
She sniffed to choose her friends
Or adopt recipes for life

That blind man I helped off the highway lane,
He wasn't blind she sniffed

I'm blind, like most recipes
Too much butter
They make butter for lazy people
Because it smells like it's good

At her olfactory best, reality has two nostrils
Even one if the other is not working
Even if a robber were to tie up her face
With a chloroformed bandana

She could smell her way through
Like people who can see through artifice
She didn't even need a nose
Because as we all know
Sniffing is spiritual

In The Same Way

In the same way a recipe for baklava
Is not itself food,
So too the voice making public announcements at the airport
Is not a person.

Yes, they are related,
Not like an egg yolk and the albumin
Not like the gram measuring cups and the flour.

But related the way
A passenger running to board the plane
Hurries along a recalcitrant suitcase
Or like the instructions for braising beef
Lying next to an illustration
In a cookbook stained with specks of past failed meals.

Cannibals

Cannibals eat first thing in the morning
Because they have no respect for waiting.
Thieves eat an hour later
When the strong sun points out
Where people have hidden gold.
Heirs of fortunes dine much later
Because time does not press.
Royalty eats by noon only out of decorum.
The righteous fast
until everyone else has finished off
all the food there ever was.

Cannibals eat themselves,
something thieves would never do.
Rich heirs prefer sweet cakes
Which kings call delicacies.
Those who fast have no names for foods.

Two Barbers Fought

Two barbers fought over his head,
eyebrows open like scissors.

Take this chair.
No, take my chair.

Two Greeks fighting the Peloponnesian War
over a hoard of Western hair
in a shop off Ste. Catherine Street
when business was slow,
until a new head entered
looking for a trim
in the middle of a battlefield.

Maayan

Some girls are made of running shoes.
But Maayan has speeding wings
That flap like feet
Through place and time.

Some girls are made of Harry Potter pages.
But Maayan has fingers
that read without grammar
and stories that end the way she predicts.

Some girls are made of stringbeans.
But Maayan tames the wild vegetable kingdom
And eats dictionaries
for supper.

Some girls are made of acquaintences.
But Maayan grows orchards of friends
That ripen like packages of raisins.

Some girls are made of blue elastics
That people twist into a ball.
But Maayan is a rubber moon
That bounces up every evening.

Deli Man

The Deli Man hung one hundred salamis every day
From the ceiling like stalactites
So that customers knew what was on the menu,
Until the health inspector said you can't do that
And Deli Man shouted how are they supposed to get hard
And the inspector whispered
You want a fine for each one I see hanging here tomorrow?

Tomorrow came
Nothing was hanging except pictures of the Mayor
Who knew salamis were hanging like dark red icycles
Next door in a rented living room
Where only loyal customers addicted to salami on rye
Could be taken to choose their poison
And feast on cured meat
As hard as a fine for a health code infraction.

Deli Man's competition Bad Deli Man
Smelled the secret mouth from the outside
Hung with salami teeth

Did you call the cops he asked,
And Bad Deli Man answered like a hero
Just doing my civic duty

Some hero Deli Man retorted,
How could you rat on a sausage?

What Happens To The Crossing Guard's Stop Sign

What happens to the crossing guard's Stop sign at night?
Is it active like overnight futures trading?
Does it still say Stop in the dark closet of overcoats?
Does it remain invincible?

I suspect it snores like the guard himself,
Wheezing out: watch how you cross,
Danger is everywhere
Hurry but don't hurry.

Stop is the only word it knows.
Maybe it would get more attention if it read,
You.
That's what it dreams about,
how to be more influential and current,
how to seize the imagination of a driving insomniac
or a profound thinker who does not know
where pedestrians fit in the cosmology

The Freedom

You had all the freedom to take your credit card and coupons
for a ride beyond the mall.

You could have found a hotel for the eager
or substituted for a hat-check girl at a tractor-pull.
Maybe you would have befriended a
down-beat accordion player
or seen a lawyer for a class suit.

Yet you chose to return
when the moon was roundest
to see if cabin fever had also driven me away.

While You Were Gone

While you were gone,
instead of changing a fuse I could have hitched a ride
on a motorcycle without a headlight,
or done midnight shift at a rendering plant.
Maybe I would have lain over a steaming manhole
or bathed myself in a prairie plague of locusts.

But like you, I chose to return.
I gave up an offer to sell roadside hub
caps and scalp season tickets
just to be with you.

We Rehearsed

We rehearsed
until my guitar strings became steel beams,
musically dumb, so heavy,
the song dropped through my lap.

And the fire truck alarms wailed for it outside my apartment,
didn't stop for breathing,
as if they were babies' tonsils single-minded on milk.

The searing cadence even interrupted
a couple's sparse dialogue at the eatery,
weighted with familiarity,
the chips moving across the table to make time pass.

The Dock

The dock of fractured planks and seagull splats
extends timidly down a dog's throat bay
that howls for the wind and inexperienced sails.

I would sit on a green wooden bench at its end.
I would kick splinters into my foot.
I would jump off the end into a net of weeds.
I would lose my glasses leaning over;
I would wash my hot face at the same time.

The winter ice will crush it.
The bay in spring will suppose it drowned.
A nearby runway of almost submerged rocks,
each coated with a more dangerous slime,
will take its place for the time it takes to rebuild.

Watchdogs

Watchdogs around the world can bark so hard
they propel themselves backward.
The energy they expel the ricochet
they feel is their human essence.
That core of voice makes them volunteer their lives
to protect metal and plastic, inedible and smell-less.

Give it up.
Stop wrenching your growling guts.
I'm here to steal in breach of laws of property
you cannot understand.
I do not intrude to cause you harm.
I'm here to keep you company
and take what should be mine.

The Family Of Worries

The family of worries
started with the woman from beyond many walls
whose son,
when angry, had a donkey's voice.
Her husband never spoke in the sunlight or moonlight;
but all their later children were orators.

The family of joys started with the woman
found in a river blocked to sift out fish.
She dried out for years
until her husband bathed her
in a stream of ointments and sauces
that made her light-humoured.
Their children were each doctors of different
liquids like oils and running saps,
so expert they could joke about their molecules.

These families mixed with each other
and with families of bargain-hunters,
of sayers of gratitude, of nostalgia,
of pantomine writers and sword swallowers.

Their progeny had no pure traceable lines
and did not care until there arose a multi-syllabic patriarch.
He proclaimed his mask, his outbursts,
his iron tears and his unused wrinkles

were the heritage of the founding mother
whose name he made up.

For good reason, he felt his leadership ignored,
and so he became sullen
and married hundreds of shy women
sitting by the telephone.

Today, purely as a generality,
families with long names are descended from worries
and all the rest from joy.

We Cry Out

We cry out as a mass of mouths in the streets
not only when dictators have to go.

When it fails to rain for a year,
when buildings tremble over fault lines,
when shrewd animals are free to stalk,
we efface all private tongues;
and stop running like the trains.

With one great surge of human cells,
in one enormous pulse of air we blow
on the horns for help and cry:
the greats have abandoned us;
the dark and cold prove they have left;
the only clothes we have are made of despair.

Out Of My Book

Out of my book of geometry
fell a spiral of angled lilies.

When I held the dictionary by the ears of its covers
hundreds of alphabets dropped on my shoes

Out of my book of pictures
tumbled many postures and a fading hairdo.

When I held the catalogue of sins by its spine
a brick of traffic tickets crashed to the floor.

Fire

His grandmother's body lay in state in the bedroom
where she was born
until a fire filling his room drove him
out to the front lawn.

He needed to cry: Save my grandmother!
Save her for what, he thought,
while the neighbours cried for him: Is anyone in the house?
No, he answered out of a smoked throat.
Just a dead person
who does not know the difference
between being buried in fire or in the earth.
Will the fire of this world save her
from the fire of the next, they all wondered.

The fire chief's neck was an engorged hose,
arriving in time to hear no answers and proclaim the motto:
Flames are an insult to home and flesh.

Yes, he saved her.
But at the back of his mind,
He hoped the heroics committee
giving out medals
would not recommend his budget be cut.

She Found A Dress

Trudging through the mall with them
She found a dress
Her best friend said was so you
And her husband asked how much.
So she wore it everywhere she could
To reward her friend and begrudge her husband
Until she found out something was going on between them.
So she burned the dress and sang the blues
To the tune of that mediocre jingle,
Always shop alone.

She Did Not Want

She did not want him to explain
why modern buildings will tend to fall down
as will moral standards and European currencies.
She wanted him to use every breath
to lavish love words on her.
He could only describe in dragging detail
what breath was
and the role of the upper palate in
forming the western alphabet.
That is why she left him without a froth of explanation.

She's Nuts

She's nuts,
panics and pukes
when the clothesline wheel creaks on its hook
like an abused throat.
The baby is new,
a mildewed doll she treats like a a slapable dog.
The family denies it to keep her
husband a patient questioner:.
Where is my bride under the bolted veil?
Why have they hidden her germs from me?
Why does she sing to the mop in the hall
And why does the baby sleep in a pail?

Is That A Frozen Turkey

is that a frozen turkey ball
or the prying head of a judge
who never gave me what I wanted

is that a wrinkled plastic sleeve
of a boiled hotdog
or the sagging gown sheer
of an over-aged hostess

is that a runover towel
in the road
or an asteroid's dirt on observatory lenses

is that anything
in the middle of a mosquito mob
or an innocent victim out for a walk
in the evening of nature

is that you or me in the still-life of a fruit bowl
or is it a mirror reflection that moves every hundred years

In My Zoo

In my zoo on family day,
I let out the caged wild salamis of Borneo,
the cunning slum bricks oddly
bobbing in the aquarium
and the cuddly lawsuits lolling on the branches

The children like to pet them;
they will not bite once they feel they are free.

It is really a device
to turn visitors into contributing patrons to
support the habitat for generations
even if I have to name
each cage and lock after them

He Checked Me Sharply

I bumped his team-mate
so he checked me sharply for the sake of unity.
I kicked him below the padding
because in 1938 his family gave no food to mine.
But he came back stick-swinging
because in 1913 my grandparent threw his overboard
to make room for beef which had no value.

He checked me sharply for its own sake
which had a better feel.
My gloves ran out of historical texture
so I punched him to make a point
which you can see in Monday's sports column.

Would You Date Aristotle

Would you date Aristotle
if he loved heavy metal rock,
if he linked prime cause to decibels
beyond the universes as we know them.

Would you have him pick you up at the door
and turn him away
if he were not punctual
if he said his ear phones caused
a shift in favour of the few,
which caused you to be lowered
in the hierarchy of souls.

Would you insist he take you to a happy club
where non-one mourned the death of Plato
where no-one thought they had potential.
And if he complained about making small talk,
would you tell him to raise a family of carpenters
and dreg cleaners most unlikely
to rise up and overturn his concert.

Rashi Said

Rashi said lame to clarify *lahat* or blade
and *appareiller* for *havva*
or let us prepare,
clusters of medieval words captured inside Bible commentary
like grapes preserved from the vineyards of Champagne.

It might have qualified him
as a native of Gaul had he not been rightly afraid
that Crusaders masquerading as hairy rats
would kill his people in the fields.

He had a different holy land and tongue.
Speaking a local language was no protection
against those who did not understand why.

Recall his opening argument in Bereishit
against they who call us thieves:
The One who made the first man allotted us our territory:
be careful whom you call a thief.

SOMEONE LEFT A BOX OF ERRORS

Someone Left

Someone left a box of errors
at the used goods store:
serving unwashed cherries to royal guests
consorting with the helper
if the wife is disabled
running over laughter in the road
while speeding in the dark.
At the bottom, ten thousand dollars for atonement.

Someone left a barrel of embarrassments at the delicatessen:
a bad word worn like half a moustache
a hand suspended for an unfulfilled shake
a thin impression that physics was easy.
At the bottom, heavy brine and cured herrings for supper.

Someone left a bin of anger in the work-out room:
lightning bolts painted on fingernails
blotchy skin on the cheek of a bald mountain
livid eyelids disguised as propellers.
At the bottom, fresh towels and socks for the gym.

Someone left a bath of upheavals in the schoolyard:
argued nothings for the next in line
torn-up computers that want no repair menus of venues
that used to be there.
At the bottom,
advice to be clean and speak if called.

What Has Happened

What has happened to yellow lilacs
floating on the river flowing tongues
I hymned for you

What has gone by,
must I watch each pebble breathing
so myself won't turn on me

See me planting my voice
where seeds sprout talking to dustmen
Grasp my throat and shake out my grave.

What has gone by
breaking up my only world order
scattering shards of my brittle song

See me soaping my mirrors,
asking where went my image
I created in your name.

Seasoning

I am scraping my thoughts against a wall
And sprouting words
Like sounds of a picket fence clicking
At the spokes of dawn.
Only snarls of sand
Smoking on cemented benches
When I tell the sun it looks a little younger
Today of all days.
And all the winds like hens
Scratch away the busy flickers of the sun From my head.

So it is nice to be in life I say
To dogs smelling out cinders
Gone up in dreams, sawdust gleaned
From the eye of the dead moon.
So I comb my curled laughing for your ears
And tell the children in the parked trees
I will hum a smirk to spring.

I Have Seen

I have seen the rise of many deaths
inside your face
and the loose nooses of flesh around your neck
have dragged away the bodies by the thumbs.
I lift up my eyes to the mountain
where my help comes from
And I see nothing but
the thin air
where I may breathe myself out of existence.
The laughter from the ripples in my glass
fills up my head like a bottle. And I cannot move myself

Because the cane you walk on is my bone.

Road

earlier we had stolen watermelon
warm from the field.
now our heads lay where the fruit had lain.
we were cornucopiae in embrace our lungs
and bellies filled with seeds.

we had spread out our shadows
as blankets
like mystics on a picnic
taking heaven literally:
one of us was fond of words,
the other talkative,
flicking coins down the slope
rewarding the hill for its company.

down in the city,
a prophet stood hugging the minaret's thigh,
moon dust under his nails caused him
wonder greater than grief;
no grief to us except our pastry melting on the rock;
we laughed,
so odd to see the sky's heart setting.
Although the missing-toothed shepherd
came to wake us we had not been sleeping
but telling fables to the flock.

When I Felt For Rain

When I felt for rain
I saw the lunch bucket drop from the fiftieth floor
gliding bread and tuna paste
and balloons of wrappers and napkins
a bird of grapes
and even proverbial apples
fell; before the rain could dampen the cake
the sweet wife made,
the workman came tumbling after

Silhouettes On Black

I

The Forest

An old man and his cold dog have passed by many times
their minds on the same bone
their syllabus of steps unaware we stand in
a coil of bark encased in sap
We are inmates of another hourglass

II

The Sky

In the air
the birds hang so closely together
the spaces between them are birds of other names
They are your knitting
placed to shade the sun from its reflection.
They are a shred of wind at last made visible.

III

my Adam's apple
hangs like a rock in a sack;
the tails of the animals I feed
are done up in question marks

The Wind Is String

the wind is string
that binds the spider to his leaf,
whose fingers become macramé-ed
by waves, branches,
hair

in a storm,
the winds are married,
woven into parasols with open mouths
that widen when the summer rain sees its chance to fall

The Bodyguard

Ready to shield the Minister's chest
he has yet to tell him of the politics of death,
fear in a shadow's shadow.
He knows there are maniacs in the audience
disguised in business suits like the one he wears.
He has yet to tell the Minister
that the Flood should purge the earth;
he has no say in state affairs;
there is no need for philosophy
if elections are far away.

The Minister has taken him
to banquets, yachts, summer homes, winter
huts, liquor parties, secretaries,
assumed him like an arm,
raised his wages,
said good-night, called him Sir,
praised him on higher levels,
asked about the family.

If he could trap assassins just in time,
he might be proud enough to say
he voted for another party.

Book-Keeper, Hospital Bed

To reason with his pain,
he converted his accounts and numbers into letters,
aleph-betting the conversion had no meaning
(what was meant by the sheet-change
the mild souring on the night table
dead stares of the visiting hour?)
He envied pain for its conviction.
In the dark,
his letters grew illuminate,
rose, gained velocity, entered his breath.
In the course of the operation,
the slit of his lips reached beyond his mouth,
words were spoken from his other throat:
the surgeon probed,
found a dove's egg in his bones
and news his aging wife was bearing children

How Could I Not Notice

How could I not notice
Someone switched my bowl of soup
For a poisoned bowl.
I notice the split-second switch of summer blaze
to indolent cool autumns.

And the flash of an assassin's blade
Hidden in my dark closet?
I can detect the movement of gleam
On the back of a raindrop before it falls.

And the flight of a grand piano
From the top floor directly above?
I can hear the whoosh of atonal wind
Made by the highest tree.

How could I not notice
The smell of fatal danger
That mixture of flame and open sky
Whether real or future
Whether I am ready or not?

Yearning

Yearning turns me into
A dry cleaner's hanger
Where I can rest the crease
Of my trousers and the pleats of your skirt.

Yearning turns me into
An unscraped dish
Where I find
the lips of your soup
And the imprint of my spoon.

Yearning turns me into
A hazard light
Where your intense redness
detonates sound in my ear.

Yearning turns me into
A renovated creature
Where you will find your own limbs
Modernized by what I was thinking
In so many years past.

About the Author

Lazar Sarna currently writes and lectures on literary and professional issues, and practices law in Montreal Canada. He is the author of the poetry collections *He Claims He is the Heir* and *Letters of State,* both through Porcupine's Quill, as well as the novels *The Man Who Lived Near Nelligan,* Coach House Press and *Book Bin Baby,* Adelaide Books. His poetry has appeared in *Antigonish Review, Canadian Forum, Canadian Literature, Descant, Fiddlehead, and Prism International.* The poetry book *He Claims He is the Heir* was nominated as finalist for the Quebec Writers Federation Award.

Sarna has lectured at the McGill University Law Faculty, and the John Molson School of Business at Concordia University. As a member of the Quebec Bar Association, he has addressed professional credit conferences and pleaded before most court jurisdictions including the Supreme Court of Canada. His numerous legal publications are frequently cited by the courts in Canada.

Thematically, Sarna's poetry veers toward the edge of the believable, gaining the reader's initial trust that what he is dealing was actually experienced. Common apprehensions, mildewing institutions, and faded love are carefully managed, reheated into a satisfying meal.

It is no secret that unique, strange and complex stories that come though the office of a lawyer form an inspirational source of poetry. The tantalizing ability to mind other people's business gives Sarna a head start in the race to capture a realistic yet imaginary world otherwise unseen. *The Tethered Man* is rooted in ancient sources, but comes alive through the painful humour of people we should know better. As titular head of a large and growing family, he is also blessed with a built-in audience.

Made in the USA
Lexington, KY
11 November 20